and His Inquisitive Dog
Guide

South Africa

Anita Ganeri

raintree

a Capstone company — publishers for children

Raintree is an imprint of Ca[...]
Limited, a company incorpo[...]
Wales having its registered office at 7 Pilgrim Street,
London, EC4V 6LB – Registered company number:
6695582

www.raintreepublishers.co.uk
myorders@raintreepublishers.co.uk

Text © Capstone Global Library Limited 2015
The moral rights of the proprietor have been
asserted.

Edited by Dan Nunn, Helen Cox Cannons,
and Gina Kammer
Designed by Jo Hinton-Malivoire
Picture research by Ruth Blair and Hannah Taylor
Production by Helen McCreath
Originated by Capstone Global Library Ltd
Printed and bound in China

ISBN 978 1 406 28111 8 (hardback)
18 17 16 15 14
10 9 8 7 6 5 4 3 2 1

ISBN 978 1 406 28120 0 (paperback)
19 18 17 16 15
10 9 8 7 6 5 4 3 2 1

British Library Cataloguing in Publication Data
A full catalogue record for this book is available
from the British Library.

[Acknowledgem]ents
[We would like to t]hank the following for permission
[to reproduce ph]otographs:

Alamy: AfriPics.com, 6, Alan Gignoux, 23, 29, Eye
Ubiquitous, 15, 24, Greatstock Photographic Library,
17, Hoberman Collection, 11, LatitudeStock, 13,
Peter Titmuss, 4, Stock Connection Blue, 16; Corbis:
Gideon Mendel, 18; Dreamstime: Rivertracks, 25;
Getty Images: Alistair Berg, 14, Bernd Opitz, 27, LKIS/
Gallo Images, 21, Lonely Planet Images/Ariadne
Van Zandbergen, cover, Lonely Planet Images/
Richard I'Anson, 12, Plush Studios, 20, Sport/David
Rogers, 22; Shutterstock: Globe Turner, 28, Richard
Cavalleri, 26; Superstock: age fotostock, 8, 9,
Biosphoto, 10, Hoberman Collection, 19, Roger de
la Harpe, 7

Every effort has been made to contact copyright
holders of material reproduced in this book. Any
omissions will be rectified in subsequent printings if
notice is given to the publisher.

All the internet addresses (URLs) given in this
book were valid at the time of going to press.
However, due to the dynamic nature of the
internet, some addresses may have changed,
or sites may have changed or ceased to exist
since publication. While the author and publisher
regret any inconvenience this may cause readers,
no responsibility for any such changes can be
accepted by either the author or the publisher.

Contents

Welcome to South Africa!

Hello! My name is Benjamin Blog and this is Barko Polo, my **inquisitive** dog. (He is named after ancient ace explorer, **Marco Polo**.) We have just got back from our latest adventure – exploring South Africa. We put this book together from some of the blog posts we wrote on the way.

South Africa
Topographical map

ZIMBABWE

Limpopo River

LIMPOPO

Kruger National Park

MOZAMBIQUE

Polokwane ●

BOTSWANA

Kalahari Gemsbok National Park

Mafikeng ●

Pretoria ⊛

Nelspruit ●

MPUMALANGA

Kalahari Desert

NORTH-WEST

Johannesburg ●

Sandton ●

GAUTENG

SWAZILAND

NAMIBIA

Vaal River

FREE STATE

KWAZULU-NATAL

Orange River

Kimberley ●

Bloemfontein ⊛

Mount Mafadi ▲

Pietermaritzburg ●

Durban ●

NORTHERN CAPE

Orange River

LESOTHO

DRAKENSBERG MOUNTAINS

EASTERN CAPE

Great Karoo

Bhisho ●

N
W E
S

Robben Island ⊛

Table Mountain

WESTERN CAPE

Little Karoo

Cape Town

Knysna

Port Elizabeth

0   50   100 mi.
0   50   100 km

BARKO'S BLOG-TASTIC SOUTH AFRICA FACTS
South Africa is a large country at the bottom of Africa. It is joined to six other countries and has a long coastline on the Atlantic and Indian oceans.

Historic places

We arrived in South Africa and headed straight for the Sterkfontein Caves. The caves are world famous for **fossils** of early people. Some of them are more than 4 million years old. I've got my boots on, and I'm off to explore the caves.

6

BARKO'S BLOG-TASTIC SOUTH AFRICA FACTS

This is the prison on Robben Island where Nelson Mandela was held prisoner. For years, black people were treated very badly in South Africa. This was called **apartheid**. Mandela was freed in 1990. He became South Africa's first black president when apartheid ended in 1994. Mandela died in December 2013. He was 95.

Mountains, scrubland, and national parks

Posted by: Ben Blog | 14 April at 2.30 p.m.

I am here in front of Mafadi, the highest mountain in South Africa. From **base camp**, it took two days of hard climbing to reach the top. Mafadi is in the Drakensberg, meaning "Dragon Mountains" in the **Afrikaans** language. Their jagged peaks look like a dragon's back.

BARKO'S BLOG-TASTIC SOUTH AFRICA FACTS

About one-third of South Africa is covered in dry **scrubland**, called the Karoo. Its name means "land of thirst." It is a great place to see ostriches, eagles, rhinos, and, especially, tortoises.

From Mafadi, we went north to the Kruger National Park where we are off on a **safari**. Rolling grasslands cover large parts of South Africa, and they are excellent places for spotting wildlife. I am hoping to see the "big five" – elephants, lions, leopards, rhinos, and Cape buffalo.

BARKO'S BLOG-TASTIC SOUTH AFRICA FACTS

Dassen Island, off the coast of Cape Town, is home to thousands of sea birds, including these African penguins. They make a sound like a donkey, so you can't miss them.

Major cities

Posted by: Ben Blog | 1 June at 3.33 p.m.

Our next stop was the city of Johannesburg. It is the biggest city in South Africa and is home to about 4 million people. I have come to the 50th (and top) floor of the Carlton Centre, the tallest building in Africa, for a bird's-eye view of the city. What a sight!

BARKO'S BLOG-TASTIC SOUTH AFRICA FACTS

What is the capital of South Africa? It's a trick question. Most countries have only one capital city, but South Africa has three – Pretoria, Bloemfontein, and Cape Town. The branches of government are divided among the three cities. This photo is of the Houses of Parliament in Cape Town.

Meeting people

Many different groups of people live in South Africa. There are 11 official languages, including English, **Afrikaans**, Xhosa, and Zulu. Most South Africans can speak more than one language.

BARKO'S BLOG-TASTIC SOUTH AFRICA FACTS

The Ndebele people are famous for their houses that they paint in bright colours and strong shapes on a white background. Each colour and pattern has a different meaning.

Today, I am visiting Soweto near Johannesburg. During **apartheid**, black people were not allowed to live in cities and had to live in specially built **townships**, like Soweto. Many township homes are very poor and a long way from where people work.

BARKO'S BLOG-TASTIC SOUTH AFRICA FACTS

South African children start primary school at the age of 7. Most parents have to pay fees for their children to go to school. School is only free for the poorest families.

Many South Africans are Christians who belong to the Zion Christian Church. It mixes Christianity with African beliefs. Each year, millions of people make their way here to Zion City Moria, the church headquarters, to pray and celebrate Easter.

BARKO'S BLOG-TASTIC SOUTH AFRICA FACTS

In South Africa, many people go to see healers when they are ill. The healers know how to use medicines made from plants and herbs to make people better.

Barbecue time

There are many different types of food in South Africa. We are in Durban, and I thought I would give bunny chow a try. It is a scooped-out loaf of bread filled with spicy curry and served with salad. You ask for a quarter, half, or full loaf, depending on how hungry you are.

BARKO'S BLOG-TASTIC SOUTH AFRICA FACTS

South Africans love to get their friends together for a braai (barbecue). Steaks, chops, and spicy sausages are served, sometimes with pap, a type of thick porridge. I'm digging in.

Springboks and war dances

Posted by: Ben Blog | 25 October at 2.29 p.m.

Back in Johannesburg, we are off to the FNB Stadium to watch a rugby match. Rugby is one of the most popular sports in South Africa. The national team is called the Springboks, after a type of African **antelope**.

BARKO'S BLOG-TASTIC SOUTH AFRICA FACTS

These Zulu people from the **province** of KwaZulu-Natal are performing a traditional war dance. The dancers lift one foot high in the air and then stamp it down hard on the ground.

23

From gold to grapes

Staying in Johannesburg, we are visiting the Witwatersrand gold mines near the city. Over the last 100 years, these mines have produced more than half of the world's gold. South Africa also has large supplies of diamonds and **platinum**, which it sells to other countries.

BARKO'S BLOG-TASTIC SOUTH AFRICA FACTS

Fruit, such as grapefruit, oranges, pineapples, apples, pears, and grapes, grow well in South Africa's warm, sunny **climate**. Millions of tonnes of grapes are turned into wine.

And finally ...

Our last stop was the Cape of Good Hope, a few miles out of Cape Town. It is a rocky headland that sticks out into the Atlantic Ocean. It was named by Portuguese explorers in the 1400s because it showed that they could sail around Africa to the east.

BARKO'S BLOG-TASTIC SOUTH AFRICA FACTS

This is Table Mountain, also outside Cape Town. It is 1,086 metres (3,563 feet) high, so I decided to climb up. Its summit (top) has been worn flat by the wind and rain, which makes it look like the top of a table.

South Africa fact file

Area: 1,219,090 square kilometres
(470,690 square miles)

Population: 48,601,098 (2013)

Capital cities: Cape Town; Pretoria; Bloemfontein

Other main city: Johannesburg

Languages: African languages; English; Afrikaans

Main religion: Christianity

Highest mountain: Mafadi
(3,450 metres/11,320 feet)

Longest river: Orange River
(2,200 kilometres/1,367 miles)

Currency: Rand

South Africa quiz

Find out how much you know about South Africa with our quick quiz.

1. Which is South Africa's highest mountain?
a) Table Mountain
b) Mafadi
c) Cape of Good Hope

2. Which is South Africa's biggest city?
a) Johannesburg
b) Cape Town
c) Pretoria

3. How many official languages are spoken in South Africa?
a) 100
b) 1
c) 11

4. What is the South African rugby team called?
a) the Zebras
b) the Springboks
c) the Giraffes

5. What is this?

5. Zulu dancers
4. b
3. c
2. a
1. b

Answers

29

Glossary

Afrikaans one of the languages spoken in South Africa

antelope an animal with long legs and horns, such as a springbok or gazelle

apartheid a system where black people are treated unfairly

base camp a camp at the bottom of a mountain where climbers begin

climate the usual weather that occurs in a place

fossil a part of a plant or animal that has turned to stone over many years

inquisitive being interested in learning about the world

Marco Polo an explorer who lived from about 1254 to 1324; he travelled from Italy to China

platinum a precious silvery white metal

province an area of a country that has its own local government

safari a trip to see animals in Africa

scrubland a dry area with a few small bushes, trees, and other plants

township a town outside a city where black people once had to live

Find out more

Books

South Africa (Been There), Annabel Savery
(Franklin Watts, 2011)

South Africa (Countries in Our World),
Ali Brownlie Bojang (Franklin Watts, 2013)

South Africa (My Country), Cath Senker
(Franklin Watts, 2012)

South Africa (My Holiday in), Jane Bingham
(Wayland, 2012)

Websites

kids.nationalgeographic.com/kids/places
The National Geographic website has lots of
information, photos, and maps of countries around
the world.

www.worldatlas.com
Packed with information about various countries,
this website includes flags, time zones, facts, maps,
and timelines.

Index